RED-HOT BIKES
TRIUMPH

Daniel Gilpin

SEA-TO-SEA

Mankato Collingwood London

This edition first published in 2009 by Sea-to-Sea Publications
Distributed by Black Rabbit Books
P.O. Box 3263
Mankato, Minnesota 56002

Printed in China

Library of Congress Cataloging-in-Publication Data:

Gilpin, Daniel.
  Triumph / Daniel Gilpin.
      p. cm. – (Red-hot bikes)
  Summary: "Describes in detail the differences between 6 popular models of Triumph
motorcycles, including statistics for each model and a brief history of the British
company Triumph"–Provided by publisher.
  Includes index.
  ISBN 978-1-59771-137-1
  I. Title.
  TL448.T7G55 2009
  629.227'5–dc22
                                              2008007316

9 8 7 6 5 4 3 2

Published by arrangement with the Watts Publishing Group Ltd, London.

Series editor: Adrian Cole
Series design: Big Blu
Art director: Jonathan Hair

Acknowledgments:
The Publisher would like to thank Triumph.
All images © Triumph 2007

Contents

Triumph has been making motorcycles for more than 100 years. The company was founded in England, and is still based there. Today it is the country's biggest motorcycle manufacturer, employing more than 1,000 people worldwide. The company motto is "Go your own way."

Proud history

Triumph bikes are designed and built at the company's state-of-the-art production plant in Hinckley, Leicestershire. As a company, Triumph has a long and proud history. It produced motorcycles for the British Army in both World War I (1914–18) and World War II (1939–45). During peacetime, it created models that went on to become classics. Those early models continue to inspire the Triumph bikes built today.

Tech talk

Employing—when a company gives people jobs.

Manufacturer—a person or company that makes things.

Naked—a class of motorcycle that has very few body panels (fairings).

⬆ The Triumph factory at Hinckley is one of the last remaining bike-production plants in Britain.

Full throttle facts

Company name: Triumph Motorcycles Ltd.
Year of founding: 1887
First bike model: No.1 (launched in 1902)

Employees: 1,000 worldwide (600 in the UK)
Headquarters: Hinckley, UK
President: Privately owned by Mr. John Bloor

Best of British

Triumph is a company that is proud to be British. The bikes it makes are the product of years of research and development. They have a unique character that sets them apart from anything else on the road. Triumph makes a wide range of bike models. The six models featured in this book include the powerful, naked Triumph Speed Triple and the modern, lightweight Daytona 675. All the bikes are produced for a great riding experience, one of the company's founding aims.

⬆ From left to right: the Triumph Speed Triple, Daytona 675, and Sprint ST are three of the six models featured in this book.

 Number of bikes sold: 40,000 per year
Number of models: 12

Best-selling model: Speed Triple
Manufacturing plants: 2

Triumph Speed Triple

The Speed Triple is a bike that screams power. It has a tough aluminum chassis that carries a potent 64cu in (1,050cc), in-line 3-cylinder engine. The Speed Triple is named after this engine.

Naked style

The Speed Triple's styling is raw and aggressive, and is inspired by the "naked" look popular in Europe. The short, stubby twin exhausts produce a sound like an angry beast, and give the bike a tough character all of its own. The tail is short and angled upward and is part of the characteristic look of the Speed Triple.

⬆ The Speed Triple is a street machine with attitude. Its styling has been designed to appeal to younger riders. This model is fitted with modified Arrow exhausts that are mounted lower down on the bike.

Full throttle facts

Top speed: 136mph (220km/h)
Length: 6ft 11in (2,115mm)

Handlebar width: 2ft 6in (780mm)
Fuel capacity: 4.75 gallons (18 liters)

3-cylinder engine

The 3-cylinder engine layout is almost a Triumph trademark. Over the years it has featured in most of their bikes. The Speed Triple celebrates this fact both in its name and its design, with the engine shown off more clearly than in any other Triumph bike. Even the exhaust is wrapped beneath the engine to prevent the pipes from covering anything up.

⬆ The twin headlights are a distinctive feature of the Speed Triple, as are the upside-down front forks.

Tech talk

Exhaust—the pipes through which the gas emissions from an engine are expelled.

Front forks—the telescopic, spring-loaded units that connect the front wheel to the rest of the bike.

In-line—refers to the placement of the engine cylinders in a row.

Styling—when something is shaped and made in a particular way.

Curb weight: 416lb (189kg)
Seat height: 2ft 8in (815mm)

Engine capacity: 64cu in (1,050cc)
Transmission: 6 speed

Top performer

The Speed Triple was introduced by Triumph in 1994—it was an instant hit with riders. Many people like its naked street styling, speed, and high performance levels. The 64cu in (1,050 cc) engine delivers a massive amount of power, and because the bike has a lightweight aluminum frame, it can accelerate quickly. The bike is also easy to maneuver and control at high speed.

Triumph Speed Triple

Short, stumpy exhausts

Lightweight aluminum chassis

Front suspension

Single-sided swingarm

Liquid-cooled, in-line 3-cylinder fuel-injected engine

Tachometer

Speedometer

Mileometer

Clear display

The display between the handlebars gives the rider important information. The tachometer—the dial with the red needle—shows revs per minute (rpm). The speedometer on the Speed Triple is just below the needle. Its digital display tells the rider how fast the bike is going. The mileometer shows how far the bike has traveled since it was bought. The mileometer on the Speed Triple is built into the tachometer display.

Twin headlights

Front brake lever

4.75-gallon (18-liter) fuel tank

Fuel tank cap

Foot pegs (the rider's feet rest here)

Fold-up foot pegs (the passenger's feet rest here)

Tech talk

Rpm—revs per minute: the number of times the rotating parts of the engine go around every minute.

Shock absorbers—devices that are designed to absorb forces and impacts to the suspension.

Swingarm—a moveable joint between the frame of the motorbike and the rear wheel.

HOT SPOT

Suspension

Suspension is important for a comfortable ride, keeping the seat level even when the bike is riding over rough surfaces and the wheels are juddering up and down. Springs within shock absorbers on the front forks cushion and smooth out these jarring movements, making it easier both to steer and stay on the bike.

Triumph Daytona 675

The Daytona 675 is Triumph's new middleweight racing machine. It was launched in spring 2006 and won new Triumph fans as well as several awards.

Daytona engine

The Daytona 675 has a 3-cylinder engine—a feature that sets it apart from the middleweight racing bikes produced by other companies, most of which have 4-cylinder engines. It is also slightly smaller than most of its competitors but outperforms them in almost every respect.

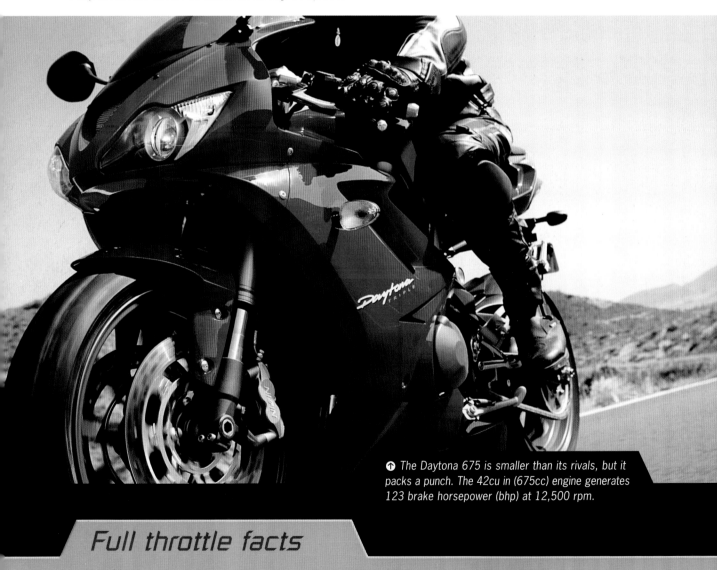

⬆ The Daytona 675 is smaller than its rivals, but it packs a punch. The 42cu in (675cc) engine generates 123 brake horsepower (bhp) at 12,500 rpm.

Full throttle facts

Top speed: 163mph (262km/h)
Length: 6ft 7in (2,010mm)

Handlebar width: 2ft 4in (710mm)
Fuel capacity: 4.6 gallons (17.4 liters)

Circuit racing

Motorcycle circuit racing is one of the world's most challenging and dangerous sports. The riders take great risks as they roar around the specially made courses as fast as they can, all the time trying to stay ahead of the other bikes on the track. The Daytona 675 is sold for use on public roads, but it was designed and built with motorcycle circuit racing in mind.

⬆ *The Daytona 675 comes in three colors: graphite, scorched yellow, and tornado red.*

Curb weight: 364lb (165kg)
Seat height: 2ft 8in (825mm)

Engine capacity: 41cu in (675cc)
Transmission: 6 speed

Ideal shape

The shape of the Daytona 675 is designed so the rider leans forward toward the handlebars. This lowers the rider's height on the bike and makes the rider and bike more streamlined. This means the bike can travel faster than it would if the rider was sitting up straight. The engine is unusually narrow and is shielded by a smooth, sweeping fairing. This also improves the bike's streamlining. Even the transmission is designed to save space and weight—it is fitted vertically to make the engine shorter.

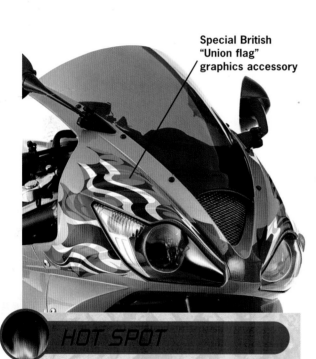

Special British "Union flag" graphics accessory

Mirrors

Under seat triple-outlet exhaust

"O"-ring drive chain

HOT SPOT

Windshield and headlights

Most racing bikes have low, sloping windshields to make them more streamlined. On the Daytona 675, the windshield is built into the front fairing and is made from polycarbonate. The two headlights are positioned just below the windshield. One headlight is tilted downward and the other is high. Riders use tilted headlights so they do not dazzle oncoming drivers, but high-beam lights up more of the road ahead.

⊙ This rear view clearly shows how wide the rear tire is on the Daytona 675. It has a very widely spaced tread pattern like that seen on track-racing motorcycles.

Triumph Daytona 675

4.6-gallon (17.4-liter) fuel tank

Right indicator signal

Liquid-cooled in-line 3-cylinder fuel injected engine (hidden under fairing)

Rear 8.6in (220mm) diameter disk brake

Pirelli Dragon Super Corsa Pro tires

Front 12in (308mm) diameter twin disk brake

Racing tires

Motorcycles have different types of tire for different uses and road conditions. Racing tires have very little tread because they ride over a flat, track surface. Racing tires become slightly sticky as they warm up, so they grip the track very well. The tire on the back wheel, which is powered by the engine, is wider than the one on the front. This increases grip because there is more tire in contact with the road surface as the bike powers along.

Tech talk

Fairing—a shell, usually made of plastic or fiberglass, fitted over the frame of some motorbikes to shield the rider and chassis from the wind.

Polycarbonate—a type of very strong plastic.

Streamlined—something that is shaped to pass smoothly through air.

Tread—the bumps and grooves on a tire.

Triumph Rocket III

The Rocket III is Triumph's largest production motorcycle, weighing almost twice as much as the Daytona 675. Its engine is the biggest of any production road bike in the world—at 140cu in (2294 cc) it is larger than many car engines.

Drive shaft

The Rocket III is a cruiser, built for comfort and effortless riding. Its huge engine delivers massive power: 140 brake horsepower (bhp) at 6,000 rpm. It is so powerful that the rear wheel is driven via a metal shaft, because a belt or a chain would not be strong enough.

⬆ The Rocket III is massive but handles well. It is a bike built for cruising on long journeys.

Full throttle facts

Top speed: 149mph (240km/h)

Length: 8ft 2in (2,500mm)

Handlebar width: 3ft 1in (970mm)

Fuel capacity: 6 gallons (24 liters)

↑ The Rocket III can be painted with custom options. This flame pattern on the fuel tank adds a unique look to the bike.

Tech talk

Axle nut—the nut that holds the wheel in place. The axle is the bar that runs through the center of the wheel.

Custom options—extra details and features that make a bike look unique.

Production motorcycle— a motorcycle built in large numbers for sale to the general public.

Custom options

The Rocket III is designed to be customized by owners, and a huge number of accessories are available for it. These range from small details, such as heated hand grips and chrome axle nut covers, to custom paint jobs and a choice of seat styles. In total, there are almost 50 optional extras for owners to choose from.

↗ The optional back rest gives a passenger support, while the small luggage rack can be used to attach a bag to the rear of the bike.

Curb weight: 705lb (320kg)
Seat height: 2ft 5in (740mm)

Engine capacity: 140cu in (2,294cc)
Transmission: 5 speed

Powerful and stable

The Rocket III is a bike built around an engine—the largest of any two-wheeled production machine on the road. Its pistons are as big as those of a Dodge Viper V10 muscle car, a high-performance road car. The Rocket III is an awesome bike, but it is one that has its weight spread evenly. The long wheelbase makes it very stable and its center of gravity is low. This means it is easy to keep the bike upright when it stops and easy to maneuver at low speed.

Triumph Rocket III

Digital engine management system

Detachable pillion (passenger) seat

Radiator

5-spoke alloy wheel

Liquid-cooled, 140cu in (2,294 cc) in-line 3-cylinder fuel-injected engine

Slash-cut single exhaust

⬆ The Rocket III combines classic crusier styling with top performance.

Electronic
starter switch

Right chrome spring
shock absorber

Tail light

Slash-cut
twin exhaust

Wheelbase measures
5ft 6 in (1,695mm)

HOT SPOT

Fuel injection

Fuel-injected engines are used in many bikes to deliver high performance. It is an electronic system that checks exactly how much fuel is sprayed into the engine cylinders to generate power. This also increases engine fuel efficiency because exactly the right amount of fuel is burned.

⬆ *The Rocket III is an eye-catching machine and turns heads on any street.*

Triumph Thruxton

The Thruxton is a classic sports bike, inspired by the café racing machines Triumph built in the 1960s (see opposite page). It has a distinctively retro look, which sets it apart from most other bikes on the road.

Classic style, modern features

The Thruxton has the look of a bike from the 1960s, but everything else about it is modern. For example, the engine is started by a digital ignition system.

⬆ *The Thruxton design harks back to the 1960s "Golden Age" and looks quite unlike most other modern motorcycles.*

Full throttle facts

Top speed: 110mph (177km/h)
Length: 7ft (2,150mm)

Handlebar width: 2ft 3in (695mm)
Fuel capacity: 4.4 gallons (16.6 liters)

The Thruxton is inspired by the bikes that rockers rode down to Brighton and other towns on the south coast of England in the 1960s.

Tech talk

Ignition system—the system that starts a vehicle's engine.

Mudguard—the piece of metal positioned between the forks and over the top of the wheel. It stops mud and other debris from flicking up and hitting the rider.

Retro—short for retrospective. Looking back toward or inspired by the past.

HOT SPOT

Café racers

The café racer Triumphs of the 1960s were the favored bikes of one of Britain's motorcycle gang, the rockers. The Thruxton has kept many of the features of those classic Triumphs, including the chromed, wire-spoked wheels, the swept-back handlebars, the distinctive seat hump, and the short front mudguard. The two color options are classic too: Jet Black or Tornado Red, with a bold stripe down the center of the fuel tank.

 Curb weight: 452lb (205kg)
Seat height: 2ft 7in (790mm)

Engine capacity: 53cu in (865cc)
Transmission: 5 speed

19

Thruxton vs. Triton

The Thruxton was launched in 2004. It owes a lot, in terms of its styling, to the Triton—one of the original café racing bikes first seen in the late 1950s. The Triton was a combination of parts from two different bike manufacturers, Triumph and Norton, and the two names gave birth to the "Triton." The Thruxton has the Triton's short, "clip-on" handlebars and a large, single headlight. Its engine is also a parallel-twin—an engine with two cylinders that line up together. However, the Thruxton's engine is larger and more advanced than the ones in the Triton bikes.

Triumph Thruxton

Centre stripe graphic

Chromed fuel tank cap

Outward-pointing chromed mufflers

Air-cooled 53cu in (865cc) parallel-twin engine

Fuel tank and molded badge

Chromed headlight and indicator lamps

Shorty-style mudguard

Wire-spoked wheel

Foot brake (gear selector on opposite side)

Chromed exhaust pipes

Short handlebars

The Thruxton's handlebars are short and swept backward, which means the rider's hands are positioned closely together. The left handgrip is fixed and does not move. The right hand controls the throttle. By twisting the handgrip, the rider can rev the engine and make the bike accelerate when in gear. Gears are selected by foot using a lever on the left-hand side of the engine. Between the handlebars are two dials—the speedometer on the left and the tachometer on the right.

Tech talk

Muffler—an attachment on the end of a motorcycle's exhaust pipe that makes the bike quieter than it would otherwise be.

Speedometer—an instrument that displays the speed at which the bike is traveling.

Tachometer—an instrument that displays the number of engine revolutions per minute (rpm).

Throttle—a device that controls the flow of fuel to an engine—the faster the flow, the higher the speed.

Speedometer

Tachometer

Left/right indicator switch

Headlight switch

Electronic ignition switch

Throttle

Horn push button

Fixed handgrip

The Thruxton's controls are dominated by the classic dials of its speedometer and tachometer. Most controls on motorcycles do not vary greatly from model to model.

Triumph America

The name of this bike gives a big clue to the place that inspired it. At first sight, the America could be mistaken for a big machine from the United States, but its heart is all British. The design is based on another bike produced by Triumph—the Bonneville.

⬆ *The Triumph America brings together classic British engineering with cruiser styling, and is a relaxed and easy bike to ride.*

Full throttle facts

Top speed: 105mph (169km/h)
Length: 7ft 11in (2,420mm)

Handlebar width: 3ft 2in (960mm)
Fuel capacity: 4.4 gallons (16.6 liters)

Brakes

The Triumph America's brakes are like those installed on most motorcycles. It has disk brakes on both the front and rear wheels. When the rider applies the front brake with his or her right hand, pads are forced against the metal disks and the front wheel slows down. The back wheel is controlled separately with a foot brake.

Great cruising

The America is a cruiser, built for comfortable riding over long distances. It has wide handlebars, a low, comfortable seat and forward-set "highway pegs," which act as foot rests on long journeys. Its engine is very responsive. A slow twist of the throttle gives great acceleration without even needing to change gear. This makes overtaking both safer and easier, because it allows the rider to focus all of his or her concentration on the road ahead.

🔍 *The Triumph America is a well balanced bike for both rider and passenger.*

Curb weight: 498lb (226kg)
Seat height: 2ft 4in (720mm)

Engine capacity: 53cu in (865cc)
Transmission: 5 speed

Triumph America

Tank-mounted warning lights

4.4-gallon (16.6 liter) fuel tank

Forward-set foot pegs (left and right) for upright seating position

Chromed cone-shaped mufflers

Comfort zone

Sitting on the Triumph America is almost like sitting in your favorite armchair. The seat is wide, soft, and padded to give a comfortable ride no matter how long the journey. It is also set very low down so the rider can easily put both feet flat on the ground when the bike has come to a halt.

Cruiser chrome

Chrome is a silver-colored metal widely used on motorcycles, particularly cruisers like the America. It is chosen for its attractive appearance and can be highly polished to give a perfect, mirrorlike shine.

⊙ *Many bikes have chrome details to really catch the eye out on the road.*

Fuel efficient

The America's 53cu in (865cc) engine is large enough to provide plenty of power even with a passenger. It is also very fuel efficient, achieving more miles per gallon, making it relatively inexpensive to run and perfect for long trips.

Wide handlebars
3ft 1in (960mm)

Air intakes
(left and
right)

Wide, 1.6in
(41mm)
"telescopic"
front fork

Front 1ft 2in
(310mm) disk
brake

53cu in (865cc),
air-cooled, twin
carburetor engine

Rear 11in
(285mm)
disk brake

Triumph Sprint ST

The Triumph Sprint ST combines comfort and top performance, and is designed to appeal to a wide range of riders.

Sports tourer

The letters ST stand for sports tourer, which means this bike offers something for both sports and touring bike riders. The current model has a sporty 64cu in (1050cc), fuel-injected engine balanced with a tourer body that comes with color-coordinated saddlebags.

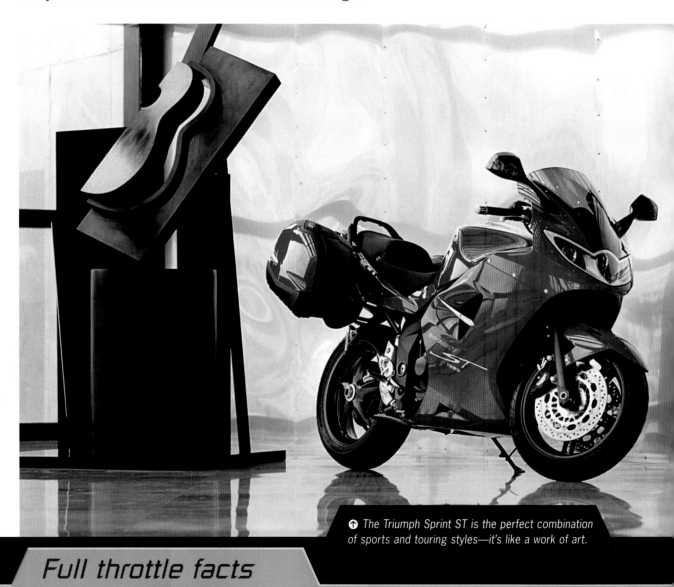

⬆ *The Triumph Sprint ST is the perfect combination of sports and touring styles—it's like a work of art.*

Full throttle facts

Top speed: 161mph (259km/h)

Length: 6ft 11in (2,114mm)

Handlebar width: 2ft 5in (750mm)

Fuel capacity: 5.2 gallons (20 liters)

Tech talk

Fuel injection—a device that forces fuel directly into an engine producing rapid acceleration.

Saddlebags—storage containers or pouches that fit on the sides of a bike.

HOT SPOT

ABS

The Sprint ST is fitted with an optional ABS—an antilock braking system—still an unusual feature on most motorbikes. ABS makes it safer to stop suddenly, even when the brakes are slammed on hard. The wheels never completely lock up when the brakes are applied, so the rider is less likely to skid and fall off the bike.

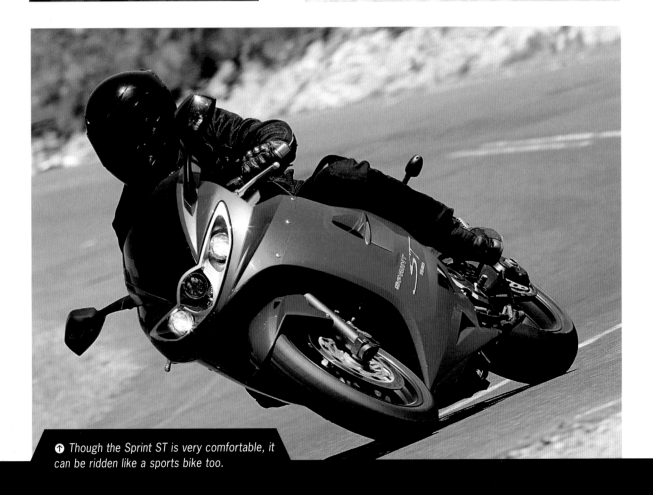

⬆ *Though the Sprint ST is very comfortable, it can be ridden like a sports bike too.*

Curb weight: 463lb (210kg)
Seat height: 2ft 7in (805mm)

Engine capacity: 64cu in (1,050cc)
Transmission: 6 speed

Mapping the way

The instrumentation on this bike is state-of-the-art and includes an LCD trip computer, which calculates journey information. Optional extras include a global positioning system (GPS). The GPS uses satellite technology to tell the rider exactly where he or she is.

Tech talk

Indicators—orange flashing lights, which tell other road users you are going to turn left or right.

LCD—liquid crystal display; a type of screen (many flat-screen TVs now have LCD).

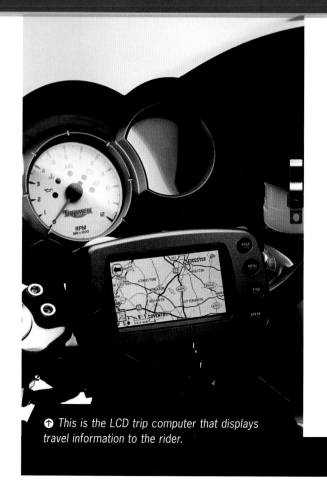

↑ This is the LCD trip computer that displays travel information to the rider.

Triple exhaust outlet under seat

Liquid-cooled, 64cu in (1050cc) in-line 3-cylinder fuel injected engine

Air duct to help cool the engine

Disk brake fluid

Indicator lamps mounted in the mirrors

Triple front headlight

Optional ABS (antilock braking system)

Triumph Sprint ST

Storage
compartment

Clutch
lever

Front
brake
lever

5.3-gallon
(20-liter)
fuel tank

Grab
rail

Large capacity

A bike built for traveling at speed over long distances needs a large fuel tank; otherwise the rider would have to stop often to refuel. The Sprint ST is well equipped—its fuel tank has a capacity of 5.3 gallons (20 liters). The bike also comes fitted with two saddlebags (see page 26) that fit neatly onto the back.

↑ The Sprint ST's fuel-injected engine generates 123 bhp.

It takes two

The Triumph ST is designed to take a passenger. The pillion (passenger) seat is built in, and not removable as it is on some bikes. Just behind the pillion seat is a grab rail. This gives passengers something to hold on to, other than the rider's waist. This is important, because it reduces the chances of their falling off the back of the bike when it accelerates.

Glossary

Alloy—a mixture of different metals.

Brake horsepower (bhp)—the amount of power generated by an engine that is actually used and transferred to the wheels.

Café racers—the home-modified bikes ridden in the 1950s and 1960s. Their riders met at places, such as the Ace Café in London, which inspired the name.

Carburetor—a device that mixes fuel with air before it is forced into an engine.

Chassis—the basic frame of a motorbike to which all other components are attached.

Cruiser—a motorcycle usually with a small fuel tank, an upright riding style, and feet-forward seating.

cu in—short for cubic inches, it is used as a measurement of the size of the engine's cylinders (cc is short for cubic centimeters).

Cylinders—the places in an engine where fuel and air are ignited to generate power.

Drive chain—similar to a bicycle chain, it is a chain that transfers power from the engine to the rear wheel.

Drive shaft—a metal rod or shaft that transfers power from the engine to the rear wheel.

Handling—how a motorcycle responds when being ridden, such as how it turns into and out of corners.

Horsepower (hp)—a unit of measurement used to describe the amount of power an engine generates.

Pillion—a British word for the back seat on a motorbike for its passenger.

Rocker—a style of dress and behavior from the 1960s in the UK. Rockers had slicked back hair, wore leather, and rode around on motorcycles in gangs.

rpm—short for revolutions per minute; a measurement of the speed of a motorcycle's engine.

Satellite—an object circling the Earth. Man-made satellites are used to transmit information to global positioning systems (GPS), used on some bikes.

Shock absorbers—devices designed to absorb sudden forces and impacts to the suspension of the vehicle.

Suspension—the system of springs, shock absorbers, and other components, directly connected to the wheels or the axles that affects the handling of a vehicle.

Swing arm—a moveable joint between the frame of the motorcycle and the rear wheel assembly.

Tachometer—a dial or display that tells the rider the speed of the engine in revolutions per minute (rpm).

Wheelbase—the distance between the front and rear axles of motorcycle.

Further information

Web sites

http://www.triumph.co.uk/

The official Triumph web site. It has detailed information and pictures of all the models in the company's current range of motorcycles.

http://www.bikez.com/brand/triumph.php

A list of all Triumph bikes produced since 1970, with links to other pages filled with detailed information.

http://www.ianchadwick.com/ motorcycles/triumph/

A huge site packed with facts about Triumph's history.

http://www.tomcc.org/

The official site of the Triumph Owners Motor Cycle Club.

Books

Triumph Motorcycles: Their Renaissance and the Hinckley Factory
Johnny Tipler (The Crowood Press, 2006).
The story of how Triumph came back from the brink, illustrated with lots of photographs.

The Triumph Story
David Minton (Haynes Group, 2003).
A detailed look at the history of Triumph racing and production motorcycles, from 1902 to the present day.

Triumph Motorcycles: A Century of Passion and Power
Lindsay Brooke (Motorbooks International, 2002).
An in-depth account of the ups and downs of the Triumph company, together with the bikes it produces.

Triumph timeline

1883—Siegfried Bettmann, a German immigrant, sets up the S. Bettmann Import Export Agency in London and sells bicycles.

1886—Bettmann changes the name of his company to Triumph Cycle Company, but it's not registered officially until 1887.

1902—Triumph produces its first motorcycle in Coventry, which uses an imported Belgian engine.

1905—Triumph builds its first completely British motorcycle, using only British labor and parts.

1907—Triumph bikes place second and third in the first Isle Of Man TT race ever held.

1939-45—The British government takes many Triumph bikes for military use.

1950—The Thunderbird, one of Triumph's all-time classic bikes, is launched.

1958—Triumph launches the Bonneville. It is hailed as the greatest motorcycle ever made.

1969—Triumph production peaks with almost 48,000 motorcycles built in one year.

1972—Triumph becomes one-third of Norton-Villiers-Triumph as sales start to crash.

1973—The Triumph plant closes down.

1974—A new company, Meriden Motorcycle Cooperative, is created with government help and the Triumph plant reopens.

1983—Triumph goes bankrupt and the brand is bought by Mr. John Bloor.

1990—Mr. Bloor opens the new production plant in Hinckley and unveils new Triumph models.

1994—The Speed Triple is launched.

1995—Triumph USA is set up to distribute Triumph motorbikes in the United States.

1999—Triumph launches the Sprint ST.

2003—The first Triumph America goes on sale.

2004—The Thruxton and Rocket III are launched.

2006—The Daytona 675 is launched to critical acclaim. The model is sold out through preorders before production even begins.